W9-DHO-101

This edition first published in Great Britain in 1988 by Macmillan Children's Books under the title *A New Look at People*

Published in 1990 by
Treasure Press
Michelin House
81, Fulham Road
London SW3 6RB

ISBN 1 85051 571 9

Printed in Czechoslovakia

50744

THE JUNIOR REFERENCE LIBRARY

PEOPLE

TREASURE PRESS

Contents

People of Long Ago

EARLY MEN AND WOMEN

These people lived thirty thousand years ago. Their skeletons were found at Cro Magnon in France, so they are called Cro Magnon people. We can tell what they looked like by looking at their skeletons. Their brains were as big as ours.

The Cro Magnon people hunted animal for food and made clothes from their skins. The man on the left is making sewing needles from animal horns.

4

The discovery of fire

People have used fire for thousands of years. We do not know how they learned to use it. Perhaps they discovered it by chance when two stones were struck together and made a spark. The spark may have set light to grass near by. Perhaps people worked out other ways to make fire, like the ways shown below.

People had seen fires long before they discovered how to make fire themselves. They saw trees set on fire by lightning.

One way to make fire is to roll a pointed stick in a flat piece of wood.

Another way to make fire is to rub a stick up and down a groove in a piece of wood. After a long time the stick begins to smoulder and smoke.

Fires burning in caves made the caves warm and kept them dry. People burned big fires at night to stop wild animals coming in.

2

In very dry warm weather woodlands sometimes caught fire. When this happened, people became frightened, and ran away.

3

Once men learned to make fire, they could cook their food. They cooked meat on beds of pine needles and made ovens from pebbles and clay.

5

Wild animals were afraid of fire. These men are driving away a fierce animal by using long burning sticks to frighten it.

6

When people began farming, they used fire to clear spaces to plant crops. The wood ashes made the land give extra good crops.

The first homes

The earliest people lived in the hot parts of the world, like Africa. They sheltered in caves in mountains or hills. The caves they chose were near water. Some caves were long and deep. Fires were kept burning inside.

Later people moved into caves in Europe and other parts of the world. Some people learned to make huts from mud, grass or reeds.

Then people learned how to make round houses from blocks of earth or animal skins. The animal bones at the bottom made the huts stronger.

As time went by, people made better huts. These people have put animal skins around simple wooden frames to make tents.

Some people still build huts with wooden frames. This picture shows a hut in a jungle clearing in modern Papua New Guinea.

Gathering food

This is a village in Europe, about three thousand years ago. The people were very good farmers. They grew barley and wheat, and kept pigs, cattle and sheep. They built canoes and went fishing in the lake.

CRAFTS AND TOOLS

The first tools people used were probably sticks, stones and bones which they picked up from the ground. Then they found they could use one flint or stone to chip another and make a sharp cutting edge. Later they improved these stone tools by tying them to wooden handles. Some tools were made of bone.

These people are using tools for different purposes. A woman is cutting up animal skins to make clothes. Another woman is punching holes in a piece of skin. Behind them, a man and boy are making animal skins into a tent.

People used flintstone to make their stone tools. They dug deep pits in the ground and chipped out chunks of hard flint. Then they broke it into flakes that had sharp edges. These tools had many uses.

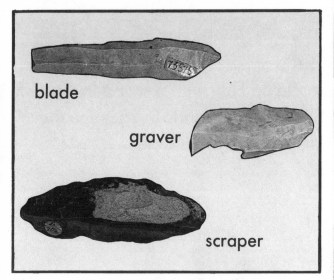

blade

graver

scraper

These are three different tools. One of them was for carving. The scraper was used for cleaning leather. The graver was used to make holes in leather.

The first metal that people used was copper. Here is a copper axe head. Later, they made a harder metal called bronze. Bronze is a mixture of copper and tin.

Men made the first tools using wood, deer antlers and stone.

First they shaped the flint roughly by striking it with a piece of antler.

Then they carefully flaked away the sides of the flint to sharpen the tip.

This flint blade was used as a spear head or as a dagger.

The first pottery

People made pots for cooking and for storing food more than eight thousand years ago. They made the pots from clay, which was dug out of the ground. To make them hard, the pots were baked in a fire. Later, people decorated their pots. At first they just made patterns. Then they painted pictures on the pots.

This woman is showing her son how to dig up clay with a wooden tool. She uses her hands to squeeze the lumps of clay into balls.

The woman rolls each ball of clay between her hands to form a clay stick. If the clay is dry or stiff, she mixes it with water. This makes the clay easier to work.

To form the pot, the woman coils the stick round and round and up into a spiral shape.One clay stick makes a small pot. Larger pots need two or more sticks of clay.

A great bath has been found at Mohenjo-daro. It may have been used by the priests.

The Indus people worshipped many gods and goddesses. This statue is of a goddess.

This cart is carrying straw, which was used for making the roofs of houses in Mohenjo-daro. The cart has solid wooden wheels.

The Yellow River settlements

Just as in Ancient Egypt and in Mesopotamia, Chinese civilization first grew up by a great river. This was the Hwang-Ho, or Yellow River. Seven thousand years ago, the Chinese began to farm the land. Besides being farmers they were also skilled craftsmen.

The Chinese were very good at modelling in clay, bronze and jade. This dragon is made of bronze.

The Chinese grew rice and grain by the Hwang-Ho River. They cut canals leading from the river to bring water to their fields.

Chinese craftsmen used bronze to make weapons and ornaments. They made bronze from lead and tin. The two metals were heated until they melted and mixed together. Here, they are being poured into a mould.

The Assyrians

The Assyrians lived in the Middle East, around the valley of the River Tigris. The Assyrians were traders. They were often attacked as they carried their goods to other lands. So they had to fight many battles. Their soldiers became very important people.

The Assyrians invented many war machines. The battering ram was used for breaking down city walls.

One of the greatest Assyrian kings was Assurbanipal. In the picture above he is hunting lions. Lions had to be killed because they destroyed cattle and sheep.

Assyrian archers fired iron tipped arrows at their enemies. In battle, groups of archers hid behind shields made of woven twigs. The shields could be moved around.

The Roman army was the best trained army in the world. It was divided into groups, or legions. There were about six thousand men in each legion. Most soldiers fought on foot with short swords and javelins. A few soldiers rode horses.

Roman soldiers were not only good at fighting. They also built forts and roads in the lands they conquered. You can still see the remains of many of their buildings.

In a Roman city

One Roman city, called Pompeii, was buried when a volcano erupted. Many of the houses were preserved under the ash, so we can find out a lot about Roman buildings. In the city there were grand houses, palaces, temples and theatres. You can still see the baths people washed in, and wheel tracks in the road.

People lived very comfortably in Pompeii. They had fine furniture and heating underneath the floors.

When Pompeii was excavated, the shapes of the Romans who died there were found inside the hard ash.

Some buildings in Pompeii were only partly damaged when Vesuvius erupted. These wall paintings are almost as good as new.

Many of the streets of Pompeii were completely ruined, like the ones in the picture on the left. It must have been terrifying when the hot ash came raining down from the sky.

In this picture the Romans are attacking a Celtic hill fort. The Romans have turned their shields uppermost to protect themselves.

The Celts

The Celts conquered much of central and western Europe, including the British Isles. They were defeated by the Romans except in Scotland and Ireland.

Today, Celtic peoples live in Wales, Scotland, Ireland, Cornwall and Brittany.

The Celts were skilled metal workers. They made beautiful jewellery. Celtic chiefs and their wives often wore gold bands called torcs. They put the torcs around their necks.

Saxon nobles held feasts in great halls like this. They enjoyed listening to poets singing stories about Saxon heroes.

The Saxons

The Jutes, Angles and Saxons came from northern Europe. They invaded Britain after the Romans had left. They set up kingdoms in England and farmed in the lowlands where the crops grew well. The most famous Saxon king was Alfred the Great. He fought the Danes, who were attacking Britain.

One Saxon king was buried in his ship. This purse clasp was found among the treasures buried with him.

The Sack of Rome

For more than a thousand years, Rome was the most important city in Europe. Then in 410 an enemy army of Visigoths attacked. They broke down the city gates and destroyed the city. They set fire to the buildings, wrecked the monuments, stole treasures and killed many Romans. The Visigoths' attack is called the Sack of Rome.

The leader of the Visigoths was called Alaric. He said he would attack Rome if the Romans did not give him land and money. When they refused, he sacked the city.

NEW EMPIRES

Byzantium

The Roman Emperor Diocletian decided that his empire was too big to rule from one place. In 293 he divided the empire into two parts. One part was ruled from Rome, the other part from Byzantium. After Rome was sacked, the Byzantine empire became very important.

Byzantine churches were beautifully decorated with mosaic pictures. The mosaics were made out of squares of coloured stone pressed into the plaster on the walls.

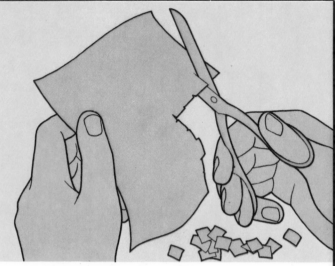

You could try making mosaic pictures. First, cut out tiny squares of paper of different colours. Or use pages from a magazine.

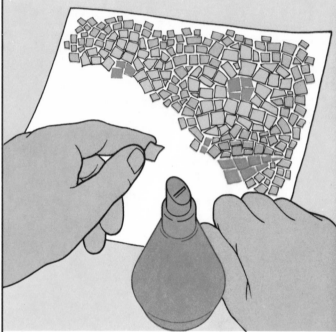

Then you can make a pattern or picture by sticking your coloured squares on to a piece of plain card. Use only tiny drops of glue.

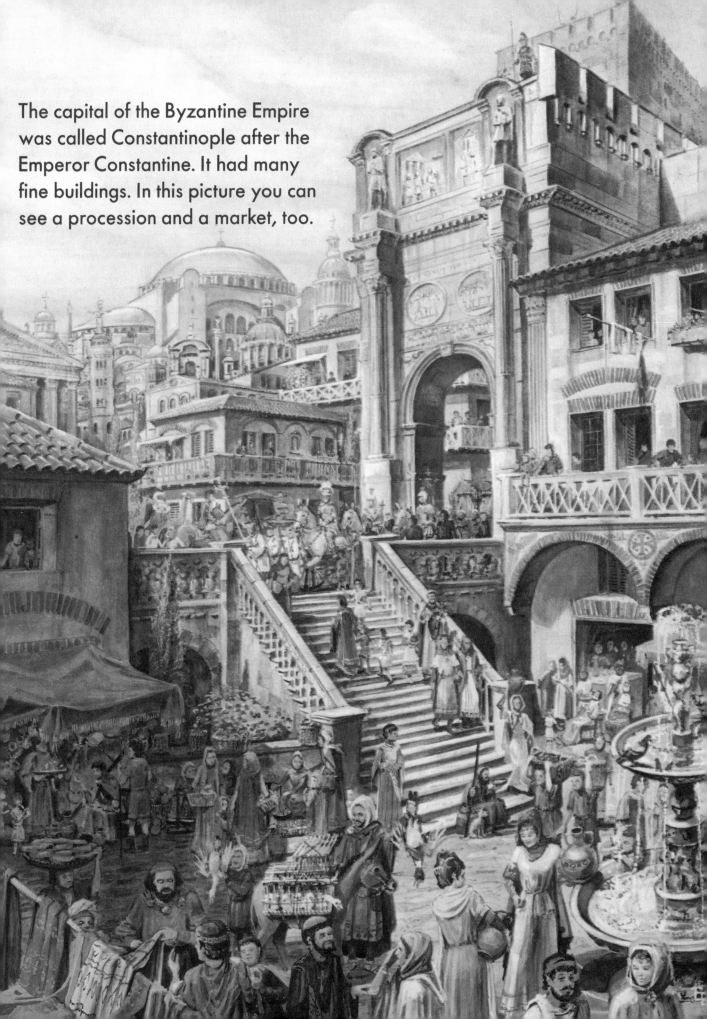

The capital of the Byzantine Empire was called Constantinople after the Emperor Constantine. It had many fine buildings. In this picture you can see a procession and a market, too.

Some Viking chiefs were buried in their ships. Some of these ships have been found. This one has been rebuilt from pieces found buried in Norway.

A single oar with a wide blade was fixed at the stern, or back, of the ship. It was used for steering.

53

hIC EXEVNT:CABALL

Here are two panels from the Bayeux Tapestry. The embroidered pictures tell the story of the Norman Conquest of England in 1066.

The Normans

The Norman Duke William invaded England because he believed that England should belong to him. The English wanted their own king, Harold. William defeated Harold at the Battle of Hastings. Afterwards, William built great castles like this one to guard his new kingdom. This castle is made of stone.

turrets

chapel

well

main entrance

DAN ESCOTT

Genghis Khan formed armies of horsemen. They charged into enemy towns, set fire to them and rode off before anyone could stop them.

Genghis Khan's armies invaded Russia too. His empire became so big that it took him a year to cross it from end to end.

Kublai Khan was the grandson of Genghis. Kublai became ruler of China in 1260. In this picture he is receiving visitors from Europe.

The Japanese

Japan is made up of several islands. In stone age times fishermen and hunters lived there. It is believed that the first emperor of Japan reigned 600 years before Christ. His name was Jimmu. Over the ages, Japan became a powerful country.

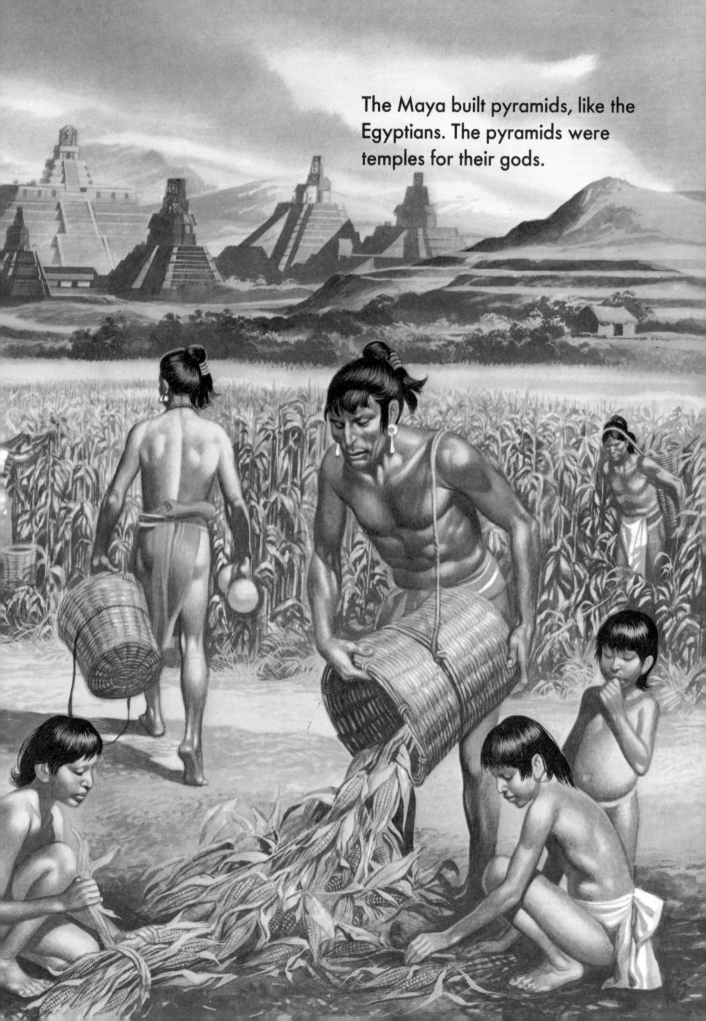

The Maya built pyramids, like the Egyptians. The pyramids were temples for their gods.

DID YOU KNOW?

The Vikings were very clean people. They wore special nightgowns and slept in beds in the walls of their houses.

A rich Muslim ruler who loved toys once had a tree with leaves made of pure gold. Toy birds stood on the branches, singing like real ones.

A Roman writer said that a spider's web soaked in vinegar and oil would stop a wound bleeding. It may sound messy, but it really works!

People
and Customs

WHERE PEOPLE LIVE

Many people live in cities and towns. There are lots of big offices and factories there where people can work. The outskirts of a city or town are called suburbs.

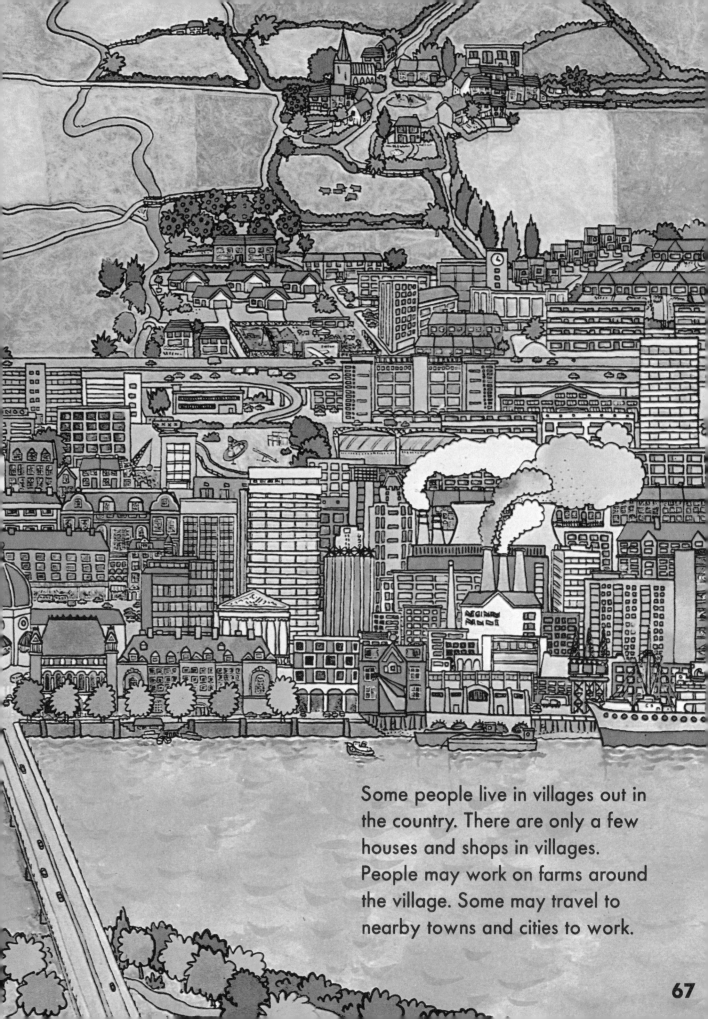

Some people live in villages out in the country. There are only a few houses and shops in villages. People may work on farms around the village. Some may travel to nearby towns and cities to work.

Villages

In very old villages, the way of life may not have changed very much for many years. Houses are often built from materials found near by. Wood or different types of stone are used a lot. In this village in India the houses have thatched roofs made from dried grass and other plants. The walls are made of stones which are stuck together with mud.

a village in India

In small villages people get to know each other easily and are very friendly. In hot places, like this village in Zambia, children can play together outside all day.

In this village on a Greek island the streets are too narrow for cars. Instead the people use donkeys to carry their goods.

This pretty village is in Austria. The people keep their houses smart and clean. Flowers grow in boxes in the village square.

Towns and cities

Thousands of people live in large cities like this one. The city provides all the things they need. As well as offices, shops and schools, there are parks and cinemas.

In a city there are many different kinds of transport. Some people travel around in cars. Others take the underground railway or a bus.

Homes around the world

Houses in each country can be made with a lot of different materials. A country also often has its own style of houses. This means that the houses look a bit like each other. They do not look like the houses in other countries.

The houses may suit the climate of the country. The house on the right is in the United States. It has a covered porch called a veranda.

These old houses are in Amsterdam in Holland. There are houses of this kind all along the canals of Amsterdam. As you can see they are tall and narrow. This means that more people can live in the city. They also have attractive tops which are called gables.

In Australia the houses are sometimes built on stilts which raise them off the ground. The cool air blows underneath them on hot days.

In some countries there is a lot of rain. In these places houses are also built on stilts to protect them from floods.

This house in the picture above is in the south of Spain.

In Spain most of the houses are painted in pale colours. Shutters are pulled down over the windows during the day. This keeps the rooms cool inside. The small balconies are a good place to grow pot plants.

Flats and playgrounds

Blocks of flats provide homes for lots of people. They take up less space on the ground than houses. The blocks of flats in the picture on the left are in Singapore. The people do not have gardens so they hang their washing out of the windows to dry.

The huge block of flats below is in Australia but it is like many other blocks around the world. In front of it there is a large open space. The children who live in the flats use it as a park and playground.

Some children who live in flats have their own playground outside. These children live in a block of flats in Mexico City.

Old houses are often too big for one family. Sometimes they are divided into several flats. Each flat may take up one floor of the house.

How a house works

A house is used for more than shelter. People eat, sleep, work, relax and entertain friends in their houses. Most houses have several rooms. Electricity provides light and power to make the rooms more comfortable. It comes to the house through thick wires called cables.

The postman delivers letters and the refuse collector takes away the rubbish.

electric wiring

electric socket

rubbish

Fresh water comes through pipes laid underground. Waste water goes down the drains. Gas for heating and cooking is also connected through pipes.

hot water tank

water pipes

electricity cables

fresh water

waste water

drains

77

Homes you can move

Most homes cannot be moved around. If a family wants to live somewhere else, they have to find a new home. There are some kinds of homes that can be moved, such as boats, caravans, and tents.
Their owners may like to travel to find work in different places, or use them on holiday.

These people live in a refugee camp in Cyprus. War has made them homeless, and now they have to live in tents.

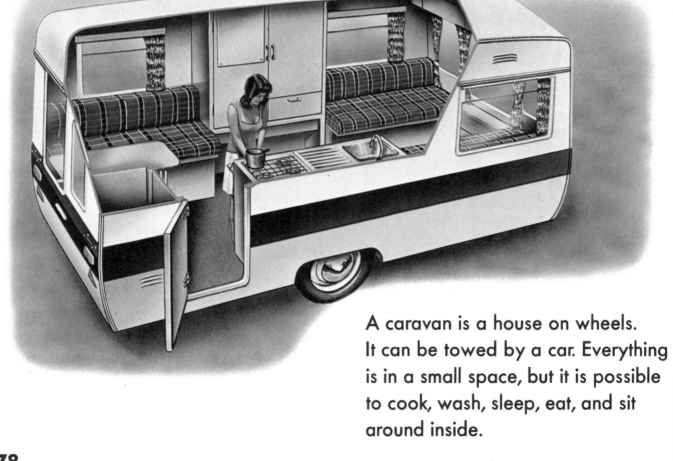

A caravan is a house on wheels. It can be towed by a car. Everything is in a small space, but it is possible to cook, wash, sleep, eat, and sit around inside.

Some cities are too small for everyone to live in. In these cities people may live on houseboats.

These houseboats are crowded together in a harbour in Hong Kong. Thousands of people live on these boats. They use them as fishing boats in the daytime but they eat and sleep on them as well.

These houses are on the island of Madeira. They are painted in bright colours and have thatched roofs which go right down to the ground.

Unusual homes

When you imagine a house, you probably think of the kind of house that you live in. The houses in one country are often the same kind of shape. The buildings look like each other. But there are some buildings that are completely different from the others. Houses in other countries look different too. Which of the houses on this page would you like to live in?

This is not really a house at all. It is a windmill which is not used any more. A family has moved into it and made it into a home.

This strange, tall house is in Suffolk. It was specially built in this way. It is called "The House in the Clouds".

The mud huts in the picture on the left are in the Sudan in Africa. The mud dries and hardens in the sun. Then a straw roof is added.

Homes of the future

We live in houses which need electricity, water, coal or gas to make things work. These all cost a lot of money. Some people have tried building homes which make their own power and heat. Homes like these will probably be common in the future.

This home of the future has a very large roof. It collects rainwater for storage and has solar panels. The panels use the heat of the sun to provide hot water and warmth. A windmill is used to generate electricity, and waste matter is turned into methane gas.

solar-heated swimming pool

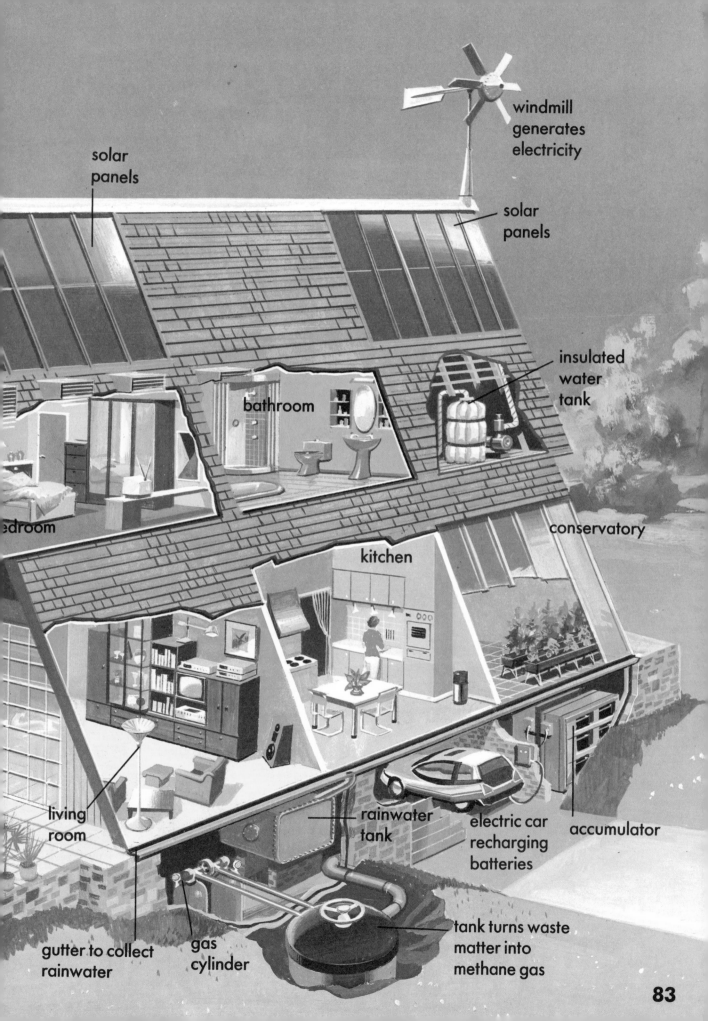

windmill generates electricity

solar panels

solar panels

insulated water tank

bathroom

bedroom

conservatory

kitchen

living room

rainwater tank

electric car recharging batteries

accumulator

gutter to collect rainwater

gas cylinder

tank turns waste matter into methane gas

83

GOING TO SCHOOL

Babies begin to learn as soon as they are born. They soon know their own parents and their brothers and sisters. They hear people talking and begin to use their voices to try to answer. Babies soon learn to sit up, and then to crawl and walk.

As babies grow into children, they learn from their families and friends. They like to play games. They learn how to use their bodies as they play, so that eyes, hands, arms and legs work together. Mothers and fathers enjoy playing with their children.

As children grow bigger they learn how to talk. They do this by listening to the people around them, and copying them. As people talk or read stories to them, they learn the words. Children can soon say what they are thinking and ask questions for themselves.

A young child may go to a nursery school or a playgroup. There children play with each other and learn how to make things. They get used to being with different people. The children enjoy making pictures with their new friends.

Primary schools

After nursery school or playgroup, children go to primary school. Here, they learn to read and write, and to use numbers. They paint and play music, and work at crafts.

Once they can read they start to use books to find out the answers to their questions.

At this school in China, the children are learning to use a microscope. You look through a microscope to see things bigger.

It is fun to make things with different materials. These children are using coloured wools to weave a pretty pattern.

Children may also be given projects to do. They work with other children to make things and find out things for themselves.

The children shown below are working together to build a dragon as part of a project.

There is no building at this school in Nepal. The children sit outside for their lessons.

Secondary schools

After primary school, children go to secondary school. While they are there they will probably find that they like some subjects better than others. This may help them to decide what sort of job they would like to do when they leave school.

Chemistry is taught in a laboratory. A laboratory is a special room for learning about science. Most secondary schools have a laboratory. Here, the pupils can study how different chemicals mix together, like the boy in this picture is doing.

The children in the school orchestra are good at music. Some of them may become musicians later on.

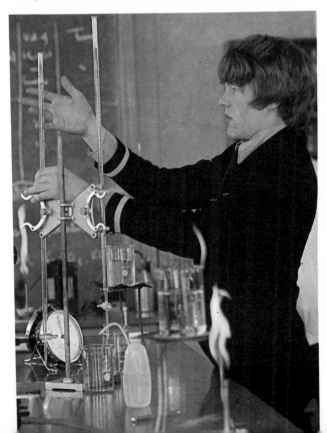

At school everyone learns the usual subjects like history, geography and arithmetic. You can also learn to make things and paint pictures. This girl is learning to paint at a school in Hong Kong. These are some of the pictures which she and her friends have painted.

The children at the bottom are studying metalwork. They are learning how to make things out of metal.

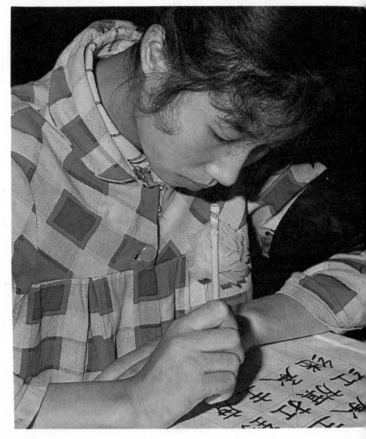

The picture above shows a Chinese girl at school. She is studying calligraphy. Calligraphy means beautiful handwriting. In China there are thousands of letters in the alphabet. They are all different shapes, so there are a lot to learn. Handwriting is a very important subject in China. It is more like painting than writing.

Special schools

Some children go to special schools. There are schools for children who are very good at music or dancing, for example. The picture on the left shows the famous Vienna Boys' Choir. Only very good singers are allowed to join this choir.

Children who are handicapped may also go to special schools.
The children in the big picture are deaf. They have special machines to help them learn more easily.

Children at special schools for music and dancing have lessons in ordinary subjects like other children.

These children are at a ballet school in Russia. In the picture above they are having a geography lesson. On the desk is a globe. A globe shows all the countries in the world.

They also have to work very hard at their ballet classes. They practise their ballet exercises at the bar, like the girl in the picture on the left. A bar teaches you to stand correctly.

FOOD

Some of our food comes from animals. Early man used to hunt animals for food. Then he learnt to keep certain animals in fields so that he did not have to hunt for them.

We also eat fish and other creatures that live in water. Fishermen go out to sea and catch them with nets. Fish farmers have lakes or ponds where they keep fish for eating.

Some people do not eat meat.
They eat food mainly from plants,
such as vegetables, fruit, cereals,
and nuts. There are lots of different
plant foods to choose from.

Wheat and rice are two important
cereals. Farmers grow them in fields
and harvest them every year.
In some countries cereals like rice
are the main supply of food.

Different kinds of food

Meat is sometimes processed to make other foods, such as sausages, bacon and ham. These all come from the pig. Milk, cheese and butter all come from animals.

You can buy whole, fresh fish at the fishmonger. Fish can also be frozen to keep it fresh longer. Some fish is smoked to keep it fresh. Some fish, like sardines, are sold in cans.

Drinks such as tea, coffee, and wine are made from plants. Herbs and spices come from plants too. Fruit is used to make jam and to flavour jellies and drinks.

The most important cereal product is flour. People make foods like bread, cakes and pasta with flour. Breakfast foods, beer and whisky are also made with cereals.

The cow is milked at the farm and the milk is sent to the dairy.

Where does food come from?

We do not buy our food straight from the farmer or fisherman. We buy it from shops. How does it get to the shops? The farmer sends the food to a central market.

The fish are caught in nets and taken back to the ports.

Fruit and vegetables are picked when they are ripe.

At harvest time the corn is cut with a combine harvester.

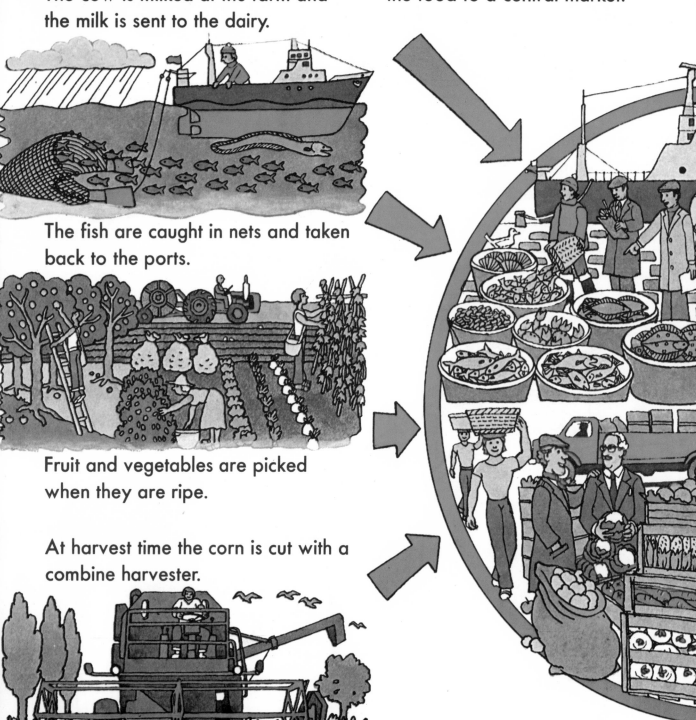

The fish that is caught goes from the port to a fish market. Fruit and vegetables are sent to special markets as well. Shopkeepers go to these markets to choose food for their shops. Corn is sent to a mill. It is ground to make flour for bread and other food.

Small food shops sell some of the foods you need.

In a big supermarket you can buy all types of food.

In some towns there are street markets where you can buy food.

Eating and drinking

Not all food plants can be grown in all countries. People used to eat just the food which grew in their own country. Now food is sold by one country to another. Many people enjoy food from foreign countries.

Countries have their own customs for eating and drinking too. In Japan tea is a favourite drink. The Japanese tea party is a formal occasion. The lady on the left is preparing tea.

Rice grows in Eastern countries and a lot of it is eaten there. This man is cooking simple rice dishes in a city street in India. The rice is made with nuts and raisins in it.

A picnic is usually eaten out of doors and away from home. If you go away for the day your mother may pack a picnic meal to take with you.

These two girls from Italy are eating pasta. Pasta is made in Italy in many different shapes and sizes. Spaghetti is a favourite kind. It is difficult to eat because it is very long.

In some towns there are foodstalls on the roadside. You can buy food there which is ready to eat. This is a herring stall in a Dutch town.

CLOTHES

Leather comes from the skins of animals such as cattle or pigs. Because it is strong, it is used to make tough clothes and boots, shoes and handbags.

Cotton comes from the cotton plant. The fibres are spun and then woven into cloth. Cotton clothes are light and cool. They are comfortable to wear in hot weather.

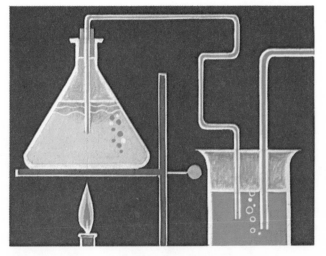

Nowadays, cloth can be made from chemicals. These 'man-made' cloths may not need ironing. They are often lighter than other types of cloth but they are also very warm.

Wool comes from sheep. Every spring their coats are cut short and the wool is spun into long lengths. It is knitted into warm clothes like jumpers, socks and gloves.

Clothes around the world

People from different parts of the world wear different clothes. This is often because of the climate. Some countries have their own traditional costumes.

The Japanese lady below is wearing a 'kimono'. This is the traditional costume of Japan.

These people live in the mountains in Turkey. It is very cold up there so they need to wear warm clothes. The women cover their heads with thick woollen shawls.

The children in the picture below
live in Lapland near the North Pole.
They are wearing the traditional
costumes of the Lapps. The clothes
have lots of gay trimmings.

Arab people live in hot countries in
Asia and Africa. They wear long
loose robes to keep off the sun.

Arabs also wear a head-dress which
they can wrap around their faces.
This protects them from sandstorms
in the desert.

Uniforms

People wear uniforms for certain jobs. You may have to wear a uniform at school. A uniform helps people to recognize what job you do. It shows that you belong to a special group. Some people are very proud of the uniforms they wear. Their dress is very smart, with brass buttons and badges. Other uniforms are more practical. They are worn every day for work.

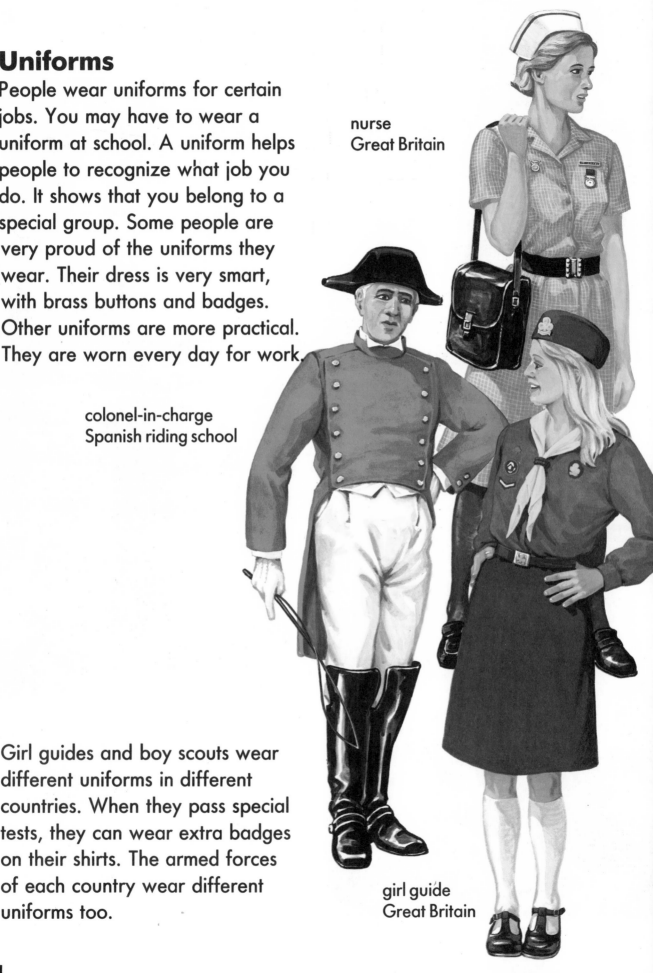

nurse
Great Britain

colonel-in-charge
Spanish riding school

girl guide
Great Britain

Girl guides and boy scouts wear different uniforms in different countries. When they pass special tests, they can wear extra badges on their shirts. The armed forces of each country wear different uniforms too.

naval officer
USA

In a hospital emergency, it is important to know who is a nurse. The nurses wear clean, simple uniforms. Airline crews always wear smart outfits. In some countries the stewardesses wear pretty saris.

motorcycle
patrolman USA

air hostess
Singapore

If you lose your way in the street you might want to ask someone the way. A policeman would be a good person to ask. You would know him by his uniform. Motor cycle police wear different clothes. They have boots and crash helmets.

Jewellery and decoration

These women live in Nepal.
They cover their arms with bangles.
Can you see their big earrings?
Some of them wear nose rings too.

Ornaments and jewellery are used for decoration. In some countries people wear them in traditional ways. This African woman and her child wear special coloured bands which you would not see in other parts of the world.

Young people all over the world are interested in fashion. Some like to wear extraordinary clothes and jewellery. Others prefer jeans and casual clothes.

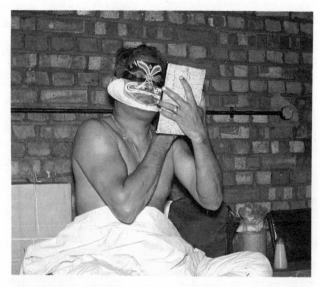

Paint has been used as body decoration for a very long time. Indonesian dancers like this man cover their whole bodies with paint.

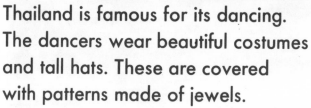

Thailand is famous for its dancing. The dancers wear beautiful costumes and tall hats. These are covered with patterns made of jewels.

RELIGION

Many people in the world believe in God, or in a number of different gods. The various beliefs and ways of worship are called religions.

Christianity

Christians follow the teachings of Jesus Christ. They worship God in a church, like this one in Greece. The priest on the left is leading a Roman Catholic service.

Judaism

Judaism is the religion of people known as Jews. They believe in one God alone and they worship in a synagogue. They say their prayers in Hebrew. Their religious leaders are called rabbis. Judaism is one of the oldest religions in the world.

The Wailing Wall in Jerusalem shown below is the most holy place for Jews. Many of them go to visit and pray there.

Hinduism

Hinduism is a religion of India. This Hindu priest sits calmly in a temple in India. Hindus believe that we have many lives. We must learn to lead a better life each time.

Hindus worship many gods and goddesses in temples and at home. They build statues of them, like this one below.

Shinto

The religion of Japan is called Shinto. It is a very old religion.

People believe in many gods and spirits. They worship them in their homes and at shrines. They make little gifts to the gods and hope to get their blessing. Shinto festivals are celebrated with processions and ceremonies.

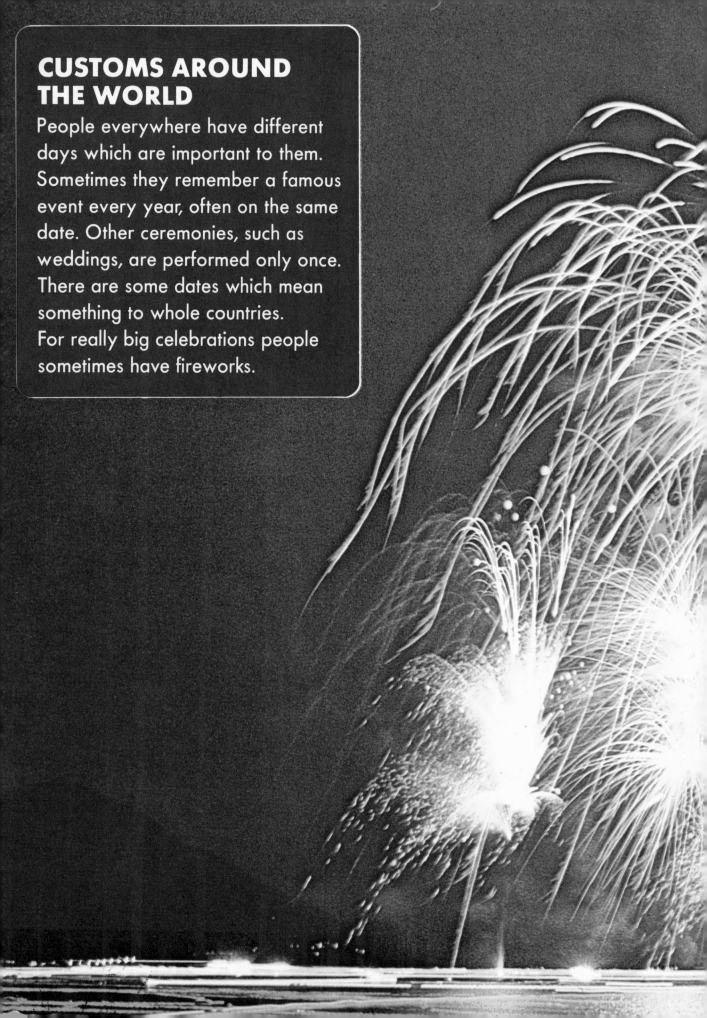

CUSTOMS AROUND THE WORLD

People everywhere have different days which are important to them. Sometimes they remember a famous event every year, often on the same date. Other ceremonies, such as weddings, are performed only once. There are some dates which mean something to whole countries. For really big celebrations people sometimes have fireworks.

Birthday celebrations

Your birthday is probably your most important celebration because it is a special day for you. It marks the day you were born. You may invite friends to a party on that day. In some countries everyone with the same name celebrates on one day.

Coming of age

'Coming of age' is a particularly important birthday celebration.

It is the time when a young person has reached the age of an adult. At this coming of age ceremony in Africa, people dance and wear masks.

The custom called Bar Mitzvah (shown on the right) is a Jewish celebration for a boy's thirteenth birthday.

17

Wedding ceremonies

Although all weddings are ceremonies to marry two people, they are not always the same. What happens at a wedding depends on the religion or customs of the country the people come from.

The bride at this Muslim wedding in India receives money from the guests. The picture on the right shows people in traditional costume at a wedding in Mexico.

A wedding may be a religious ceremony, in a church. A lot of weddings do not take place in a church, and these do not have any religious customs. All weddings mark the bond between the two people. In a Christian wedding, the groom gives the bride a ring. In the Japanese wedding shown here, the couple sip cups of wine.

This picture of a village wedding shows a Swedish custom. A band leads a procession of the people taking part.

Funerals

A funeral is a religious ceremony which is held when someone dies.

People are usually buried in a holy place like a churchyard. In some countries the family and friends wear black at a funeral to show their sadness. Other funerals are bright parades. This brightly painted box is a Chinese coffin. At a grave in Indonesia, statues of the dead person's ancestors watch over the burial place.

This gay procession in Bali, Indonesia, is also a funeral. The coffin is put inside the statue of a bull and carried through the streets.

Christmas

At Christmas Christians all over the world celebrate the birth of Jesus Christ. They give each other presents and decorate a tree.

Children hang up stockings and St Nicholas, the patron saint of children, fills them with presents. In the Netherlands he has young helpers dressed as black boys.

There are some strange customs which people have followed for many years at Christmas time and New Year. Look at the funny things which these people are doing. Do you follow any of these customs?

New Year

The beginning of each New Year is celebrated in most countries.

On New Year's Eve some people go to church. Others invite friends round to their homes. When the clock strikes midnight they all welcome the New Year together. The Chinese New Year begins on a different date.

Unusual customs

Most countries have their own customs which are not seen anywhere else. Many of these ceremonies have been performed for a long time.

This African man is walking on stilts. He is taking part in a ceremony for chasing away evil spirits.

Every year on December 6th, people in Switzerland dress up in big hats with candles inside, as you can see in the picture below.

The picture on the left shows some children doing maypole dancing. Maypole dancing is an old custom which you can still see in country parts of Britain. As the people dance around the maypole, they hold coloured ribbons. The ribbons wind around the pole in a pattern.

Carnivals happen all over the world. People dress up and parade through the streets. There are bands playing music, and people dance. Sometimes whole towns join in. The costumes are bright and strange, like this one from Trinidad.

DID YOU KNOW?

Not many people live to be 100. We know of at least one person who lived to be 113.

One of the cleverest children who ever lived was called Wolfgang Mozart. He lived in Austria about 200 years ago. He wrote his first symphony when he was only five.

The heaviest man ever known lived in America. He weighed 171 kilos (27 stones) when he was only 10. When he was grown up he weighed 485 kilos (76 stones). His waist measured about 3 metres (10 feet). Imagine how big his clothes must have been. How many people do you think could get into a pair of his trousers?

What People Do

WORKING IN SHOPS

The shops in this picture are in a place called a shopping 'precinct'. No cars are allowed on the street, so you do not have to worry about crossing the road. This makes shopping much easier. You can wander around, looking at the shops and deciding what to buy.

The baker sells bread and cakes. The butcher is standing outside his shop. He sells meat. Can you see the greengrocer? He sells fresh fruit and vegetables of all kinds.

129

The baker

You can buy fresh loaves of bread in the baker's shop. Sometimes the loaves are still warm from the oven when you buy them. Nowadays, most bread is made in factories and then taken to shops. Some bakers still bake their own bread. Then it is fresh, and good to eat.

First the baker mixes the dough. He uses flour and water and yeast. Yeast makes the bread 'rise'. If the baker did not put yeast into the dough, the loaves would be flat.

When the dough has been mixed, the baker takes it out of the bowl and kneads it. He turns the dough over and over, folding it and pushing it. This spreads the yeast out well.

The baker shapes the loaves before baking them. He makes both big and small loaves. Many bakers also make round loaves and cottage loaves.

The baker leaves the loaves to 'rise'.
When they are the right size, the
baker puts them in the oven.
He leaves them there until they are
brown and crusty on top.

The bread is ready. The baker takes
it out of the oven and leaves it to
cool for a while. Then he takes the
bread into the shop. It is still warm
and smells delicious.

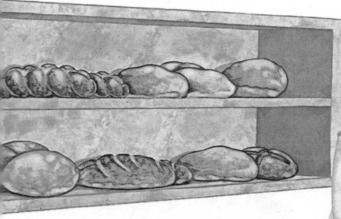

In the shop, customers can choose
from many different kinds of bread.
They can buy white or brown bread.
They can also buy loaves in different
shapes. Some bakers also sell
croissants, pastries and cakes.

The hairdresser

Hairdressers work in shops called salons. Customers go to a salon to have their have cut, or washed and set. Sometimes they ask the hairdresser to give them a new hair style. Some salons have departments for men and women. Shops which are just for men's hairdressing are called barbers' shops.

The hairdresser is shampooing a customer's hair. She washes it with shampoo and then rinses it.

Hairdressers sometimes use a conditioner to keep the hair healthy. They can also use dyes to make people's hair a different colour.

Hairdressers usually cut hair when it is wet.

Some customers like their hair curled. The hairdresser winds the hair around rollers while it is wet.

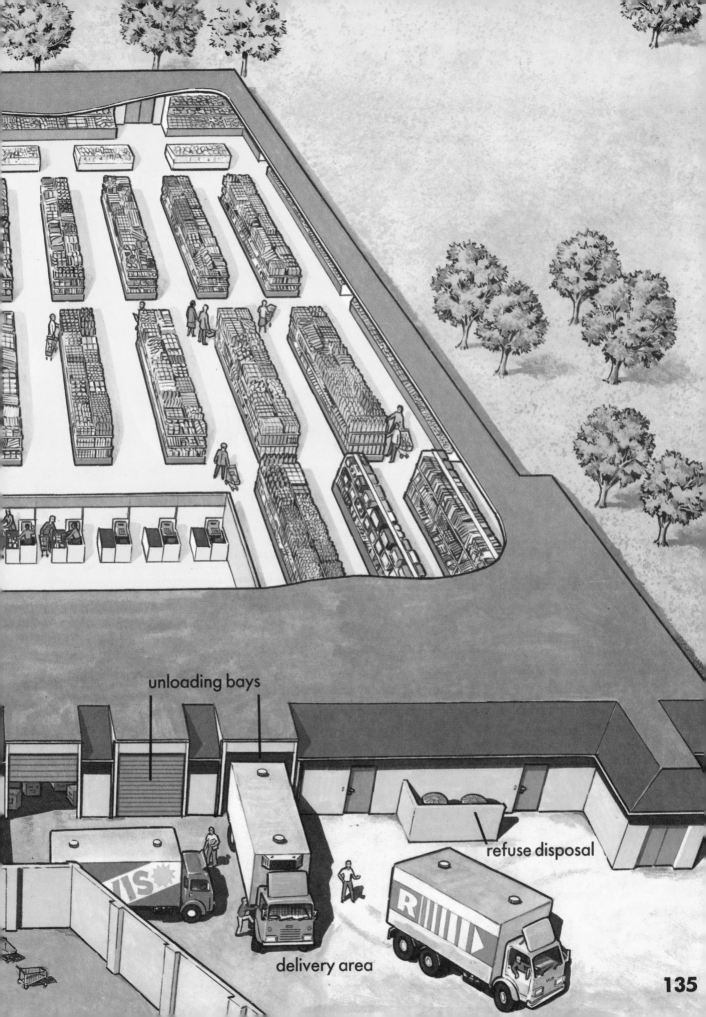

unloading bays

refuse disposal

delivery area

WORKING ON THE LAND

Farmers supply most of the food that we eat. Some farmers keep animals such as sheep and cattle to provide milk and meat. Other farmers grow fruit, vegetables and crops such as wheat, barley and rye.

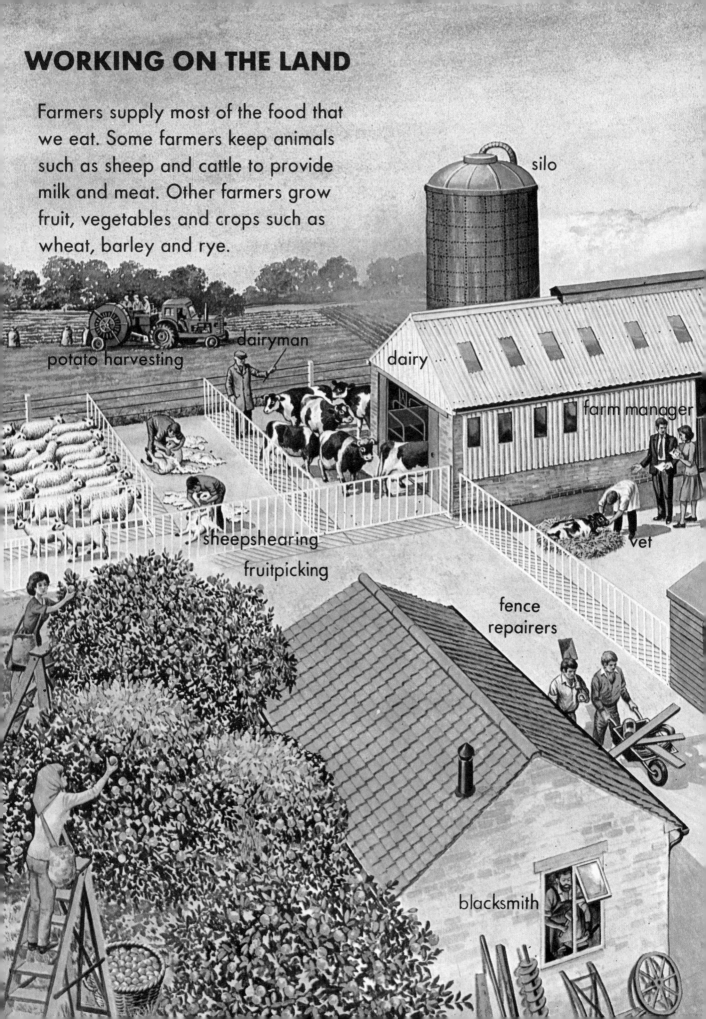

silo

dairyman

potato harvesting

dairy

farm manager

sheepshearing

fruitpicking

vet

fence repairers

blacksmith

cropspraying

Lots of people work on this large farm. They pick the fruit and vegetables, milk the cows, shear the sheep and harvest the corn. Farmers have to work very hard.

office

farmhouse

haymaking

collecting milk

Animal farming

Certain animals are very important to us. They provide us with things we need to live. Animals like this are called 'domesticated' because they are no longer wild. We get milk from cows and wool from sheep.

In Australia many cattle stations are so big that the cattle have to be rounded up by men on horses. Sometimes the cattle are taken many miles to find good grazing land. These farms are called ranches.

ostrich

reindeer

llama

Oysters are a kind of shellfish.
Many people like to eat them.
On this oyster farm the oysters are
being collected from the 'beds'.

In other parts of the world different animals are domesticated. In Lapland it is very cold. People who live there keep reindeer to pull sledges and to give them milk. In the desert it is very hot. Camels can store water so they are used for travel. In South America llamas are kept to provide wool and meat. Llama wool is very silky. Some people breed pheasants for their meat.

pheasant

In the winter sheep grow thick woolly coats to keep them warm. They have to be dipped in a special liquid. This liquid keeps their coats clean and keeps their skins healthy.

Crop farming

Farmers grow grain crops such as barley and wheat. First the farmer ploughs the field. He turns the soil over, as if he were digging the garden. This breaks up the soil.

Next, the seeds are sown. This is often done by a machine. The machine sprinkles the seeds in rows. Not all the seeds will grow.

Some of the seeds will be eaten by birds and some will die, so the farmer plants more than he will need. When the seeds begin to grow, small green plants appear. They need plenty of sun and rain to grow into strong, healthy plants. Barley and wheat turn yellow when they are ripe.

When the crops are ready they are picked. This is called 'harvesting'. Barley, wheat and other cereal crops are gathered with a combine harvester. This cuts down the plants. Then it separates the grain or 'ears' from the stalks. The stalks are made into straw bales. Grain is put in sacks.

Some straw is kept for animals to sleep on in the winter. The grain is sent to the mills. In the mills it is made into flour for bread and cakes.

Gardening

Many people enjoy gardening. They do it when they are not working. They grow vegetables and flowers for their families. Some people look after gardens as a job. Big gardens need several gardeners. They keep the flower beds and vegetable garden tidy. They also put in new plants all the year round. Many gardeners also work in parks.

Nurseries are places where plants and flowers are grown. Many plants are grown in greenhouses so that they will not die in the winter. People go to nurseries to buy plants to put in their own gardens. Florists buy cut flowers. Holland is famous for its fields of tulips.

Working with trees

Trees are specially planted in places called tree plantations. Foresters plant the trees and look after them. Sometimes trees have to be cut down for timber. This is called felling. Foresters cut down the trees with big chain saws. The wood is used to make furniture and other goods.

WORKING AT SEA

Many people work at sea. There are
jobs to be done on different kinds of
boats. The big ship is a passenger
ferry, which takes people from one
place to another. Fishermen go out in
trawlers to catch fish. Submarines
can dive beneath the waves and
travel underwater. In some jobs
people stay at sea for a long time.

passenger ferry

trawler

submarine

People work at sea in other ways too.
They build rigs to drill for oil from
the ocean bed. Astronauts sometimes
land on the sea. They are let out of
their space capsule by frogmen.
Lighthouses warn of the danger of
rocks. If a boat sinks, its crew can be
rescued by lifeboat or helicopter.

helicopter

oil
rig

lighthouse

space
capsule

lifeboat

70-001

The fisherman

Most of the fish we eat comes from the sea. Fishermen go out to sea in boats to catch them. Sometimes boats stay at sea for several days. The big picture on the right shows fishermen in the Seychelles. They are fishing with a seine net. This is a big net with floats around the top. This net can be used from the shore.

Fishermen unload their fish at seaside towns. These towns are called fishing ports. They are usually in sheltered bays with a harbour. Boats are moored in the harbour at night, or when the weather is bad.

The captain of a large fishing boat has to navigate the boat to the fishing grounds. He finds a good place to fish by looking for green water. Fish eat tiny animals called plankton. These animals make the water green. When the captain sees the green water, he knows it is a good place to fish.

When the captain has found a good place to fish, the crew get the nets ready. The nets spread out from the boat. Sometimes nets go right down to the bottom of the sea. The crew wait till the nets are full.

Have you ever eaten fresh fish? In some seaside towns fishermen catch fish and sell it the same day. People buy the fish and cook it. It tastes delicious.

The Merchant Navy

People in the Merchant Navy work on ships that carry cargo or passengers. This ship is carrying cargo to another country. The cargo is stored in the middle and the front of the ship. Some of the crew are tying the cargo to the deck to keep it secure. Other members of the crew are working in the engine room, eating or sleeping.

1. The captain on the bridge
2. The navigator studying charts
3. The radio operator
4. The crew in the engine room

Working on a lifeboat

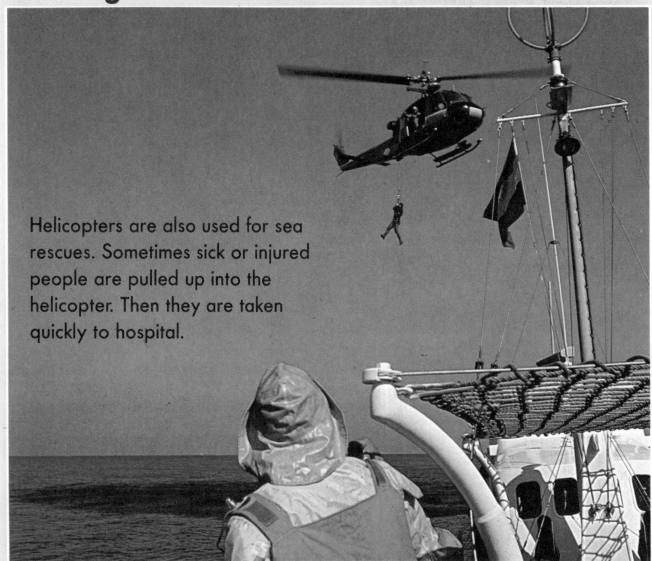

Helicopters are also used for sea rescues. Sometimes sick or injured people are pulled up into the helicopter. Then they are taken quickly to hospital.

Most seaside towns have a lifeboat. Lifeboatmen are usually volunteers. This means that they have another job as well. They have to be ready to leave their job and go out to sea when a ship is in danger. The sea is very rough when they go out.

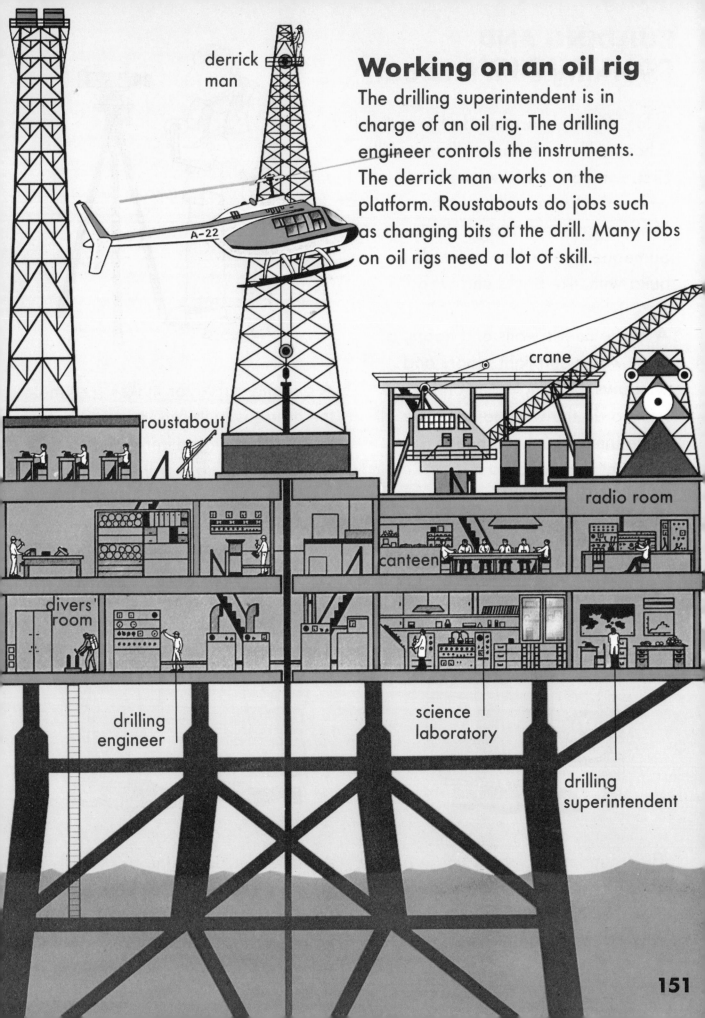

derrick man

roustabout

Working on an oil rig

The drilling superintendent is in charge of an oil rig. The drilling engineer controls the instruments. The derrick man works on the platform. Roustabouts do jobs such as changing bits of the drill. Many jobs on oil rigs need a lot of skill.

crane

radio room

canteen

divers' room

drilling engineer

science laboratory

drilling superintendent

151

BUILDING AND CONSTRUCTION

A lot of people are needed to build a house. They all have different skills. First, someone chooses the land where the house will be built. Then an architect designs the house. Someone else orders materials to build with, like bricks and wood.

A house needs walls and floors, a roof, water and light, doors and windows. No single person knows how to do the work to complete all these things. Each job needs a different person to do it.

A quantity surveyor makes sure that the house is built properly. He finds people to do the different jobs and works out the cost of the materials.

The 'foundations' of the house are underground. Men dig trenches and then fill them in with concrete to support the house.

A bricklayer builds the brick walls. He stands on 'scaffolding' to build the high parts. Carpenters put in the wooden parts such as floor boards.

The architect works closely with the surveyor. She designs the house and prepares drawings which show both the inside and the outside.

Before work can begin, the ground has to be cleared. A bulldozer is used to flatten the land. The driver makes sure the land is flat.

The plumber lays pipes so that the house has a supply of water. The electrician makes sure that the lights and heating work properly.

Last of all, the house is painted by decorators. They paint the walls and woodwork to protect them and make them look nice.

The building site

bricklayer

carpenter

plumber

154

Here you can see all the people working on a house. Look at the cement mixer. When the cement is ready the bricklayer uses it to stick the bricks together. One man is carrying the bricks to the bricklayer. He carries them in a 'hod'. The men putting tiles on the roof are called tilers. Plumbers are fitting the radiators inside the house.

tiler

electrician

decorator

bulldozer

cement mixer

quantity surveyor

155

Engineering

Engineers work out the best way to make things. Some engineers make things that move, like aeroplanes, ships, cars, railway engines and rockets for going into space. Some engineers find ways of improving machines. They work out how to save fuel and how to make machines work faster.

Some engineers work on buildings. They are called civil engineers. They make sure that the right machines and materials are used, so that the building will not fall down. The engineer in the picture above is working on an enormous block of offices. He is studying the plans of the building.

In the big picture you can see some of the things that engineers do. They build bridges and roads as well as buildings and factories. Have you seen one of the huge suspension bridges that span wide rivers and estuaries? Engineers plan them so that they are safe for traffic. They also design machines.

This engineer is using a 'walkie talkie'. This is a small radio used to talk to people near by. The engineer is working on a building. He has to talk to men who are high up on the scaffolding, to tell them what to do. His hard hat protects him.

nurse

canteen

office manager

designing

foreman

FACTORIES AND OFFICES

Working in a factory

Most of the things we use everyday are made in factories. The factories are specially organized so that a lot of the same sort of things can be made very quickly. This factory makes bicycles.

testing

welding

production line

store

People in factories see the nurse if they are ill. They eat in the canteen. In the design studio new kinds of bicycles are planned. A sample bicycle is made and tested to make sure there is nothing wrong with the design. Different parts of the bicycle are made in the welding room.

The production line

Machines are often put together on production lines. Cars are normally built in this way. They are not built one by one, but passed along a line so that the various parts of the car can be fitted together. Each job, such as welding, screwing and drilling, must be done hundreds of times each day. Some jobs are done by people. Others are done by automatic machines or 'robots'.

The car soon takes shape on the production line. One of the most important jobs to be done is the painting. Paint protects the metal from rust.

The man working in this factory in Germany is using a machine to make embroidered ribbon. The ribbons will be used to decorate clothes.

Working with clothes

Clothes are made from many different types of material. Cotton is made from cotton plants. Wool comes from sheep. Other materials, such as nylon, are made by men. The nylon is made in factories. In the picture below a Thai woman is preparing silk.

Designers draw patterns for the clothes. The material is then cut out. The pieces are sewn together with sewing machines. These women are making dresses in a factory in Brazil.

Clothes are sold in shops and also in boutiques. Shop assistants help customers to find clothes that are the right size and that look nice.

Working in an office

This is an open-plan office. All the people work in a big open space. The boss, however, has her own office. The receptionist sits at the entrance to the office. When visitors come she shows them where to go. Two visitors are waiting for the boss.

telephonist

164

Secretaries type letters, answer the phone and file away letters.
The telephonist answers the phone. She switches the calls through to the right people by using the switchboard.

boss

receptionist

secretary

165

Start here

1

2

3

4 5 6 7

Bottom falls out of dustbin
Go back 1

SERVICES

We often meet the people you can see in this game. They all do jobs that help us in some way. You may see some of them on your way to school. Perhaps you will see a postman, or a policeman on road duty.

Collect pencil case from Lost Property
Move on 3

Knock over librarian's books
Go back 6

47 46 45 44 43 42 41 40 39 38

48

49 Hurt your arm
Back 1

Doctor mends arm
Move on 3

Taxi driver takes you home to finish

50 51 52 53 54 55 56 57 58

Firemen have to train a lot before they are ready to go to fires. There are big ladders on fire engines. Firemen practise using the ladders, so that they can rescue people trapped on high buildings.
Firemen do not only put out fires. They help during floods, too.

The postman

The postman's job is to see that letters and parcels go to the right places. Some postmen collect letters. Other postmen deliver letters. What happens when you post a letter in a pillarbox or when you take a parcel to the post office?

First, the postman collects all the letters and parcels. He takes them to the sorting office.

The letters have to be sorted, so that they go to the right places. Machines can help to do this.

Mail goes by train to the towns. Then it is taken to the post office.

In the post office the letters are sorted. Here, people are sorting the letters into boxes. Then the letters are put in sacks.

The postman collects the letters from the post office. He brings the mail to your house.

The dustman

The dustman takes away rubbish from the streets and from our homes. He goes to all the houses and collects the dustbins. Then he empties the rubbish into a lorry.

The lorry takes the rubbish to a place called a 'tip'. These tips are usually out of the centre of towns. Sometimes the rubbish is burnt. Dustmen often work early in the morning, before many people are up.

The teacher

Teachers in primary schools teach all subjects. In secondary schools, teachers usually teach only one subject. They have to know all about their subject and help their children to understand what they learn.

The class in the picture on the right is in Sri Lanka. The weather in Sri Lanka is hot, so the teacher can teach some lessons outside.

Some teachers teach subjects like games, music and dancing. This dancing lesson is taking place in a school in North Africa.

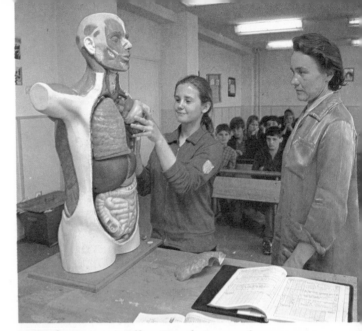

Teachers usually work in a classroom. This lesson is about how the body works. The teacher is using a model to show the different parts of the body. The children have to learn the names of the different parts and where they are found.

The librarian

A library is a place where people can go to borrow books. They can study in the library, too. So they can use lots of different books without having to take them home. Many schools have libraries.

A librarian is someone who looks after a library. Librarians keep a record of everyone who borrows books. They know a lot about the books and can give people advice and answer their questions.

Working in a hospital

When you are ill you sometimes have to go to hospital. The people who work in hospitals have learnt all about illness. They know how to help sick people get better. Doctors and nurses work in hospitals. There are other people working there too.

This boy has fallen and hurt his leg.
A man is giving him first aid.
He keeps the boy still, so that he will not hurt himself any more.

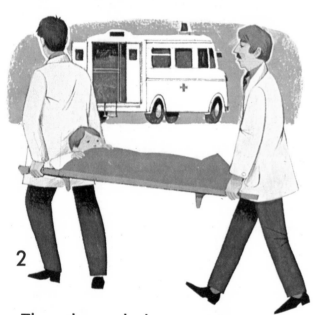

The doctor at the hospital goes to see the boy. He examines the boy's leg and finds that it is broken.

Then the ambulance arrives.
The ambulance men put the boy on a stretcher. Then they drive him to the nearest hospital.

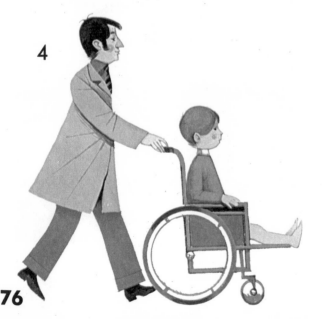

The boy cannot walk because his leg hurts. The porter comes along with a wheelchair. He wheels the boy to the ward.

176

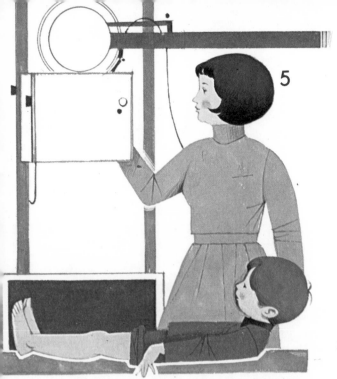

The radiographer x-rays the boy's leg to find out how the bone is broken. An x-ray is a picture of the inside of the body. It shows the bones and the parts between them.

The doctor decides to put the leg in plaster. This will keep the leg straight, so the bone can set.

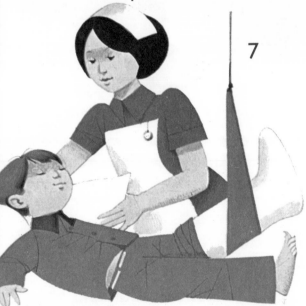

While the boy is in the ward he is looked after by a nurse. She makes sure that he is comfortable. She will bring him meals, too.

After a few days the boy gets out of bed. His leg is stiff from being in plaster. A physiotherapist help him to exercise it.

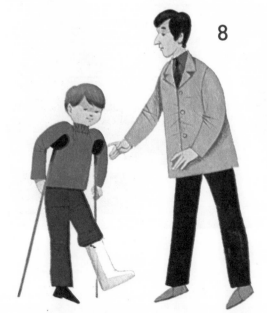

The doctor

In parts of Australia the towns are far apart. The doctor may live a long way away. He goes by plane to see his patients, so he is called the 'flying doctor'.

Not all doctors work in hospitals. Many doctors see their patients in the 'surgery'. A surgery is a place where people can go if they are ill but do not need to go to hospital.

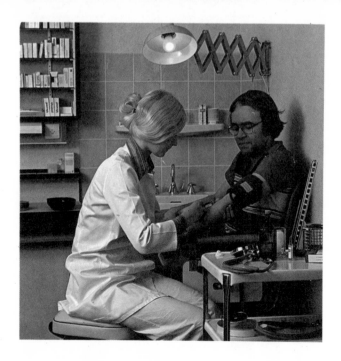

The doctor sees her patients and finds out what is wrong with them. Then she tells them what kind of medicine will make them better. Sometimes doctors give injections. An injection stops you from catching a disease.

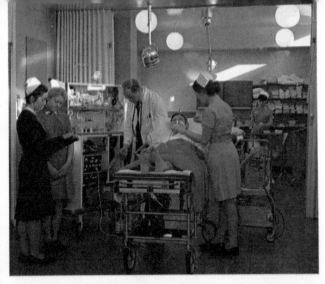

The nurse

Nurses usually work in hospitals. They look after people who are ill in bed. Nurses give their patients medicine and make them comfortable. If a patient cannot breathe properly, a nurse will give him oxygen to help him get better.

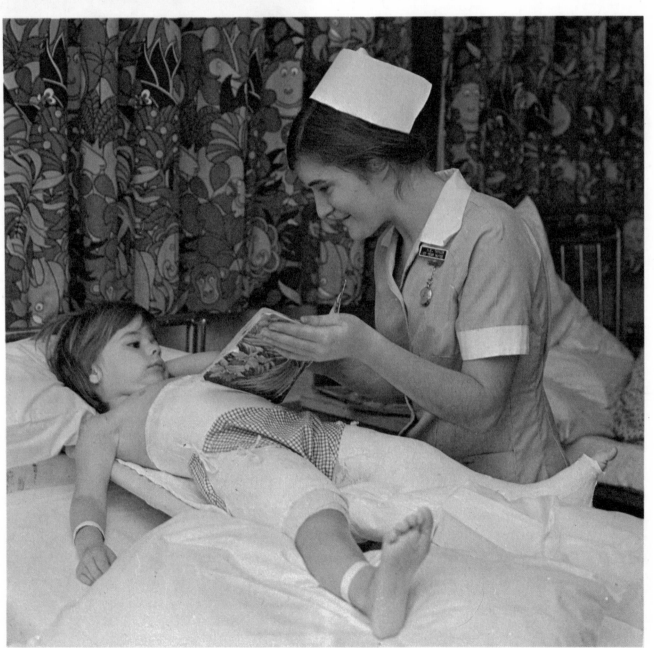

The scientist

All scientists try and discover more about the way things work and why things happen. Some scientists do experiments to find new medicines and new types of food. Other scientists study the past. They try to find out how life began. Some scientists study how people lived a long time ago.

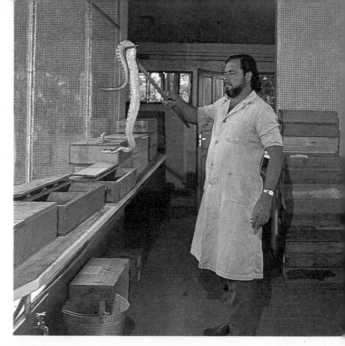

Scientists need to find out whether new medicines will work. They use animals to help them with their experiments. In the picture on the left, a snake is being used.

Archaeologists find remains of old buildings. They study them to see how people lived a long time ago.

This scientist is in her laboratory. She is experimenting with chemicals in test tubes. She is studying what happens to the chemicals.

Scientists study the weather too. They use instruments to measure rainfall, sunshine, wind and clouds.

Working with money

Everyone needs money. Without money you cannot buy the things you need to live, such as food and clothes. Money can be banknotes or coins. It is made in a place called the mint. The mint produces all the money that is made in a country. No one else can make coins.

New money is taken to banks to be kept safely. Security men take it there so that it will not be stolen on the way. They travel in special vans.

Many people keep the money that they earn in a bank. The bank keeps their money safe until they want it. Then they go and cash a cheque from the cashier. They can cash just the amount of money they need to buy things.

Customers pay the shopkeeper
when they buy things in his shop.
The shopkeeper puts all the
money that he takes into a till.

At the end of the day, the shopkeeper
counts up all the money in the till.
Then he takes it along to the bank.
He does this every day. Most
businesses keep their money in
banks, not in their offices.

The shopkeeper pays in the money
to the cashier. The cashier counts it
all out and writes down the amount.

Working on a newspaper

Working on a newspaper is a very busy job. Many newspapers are printed each day, and they have to have all the latest news in them. The editor is in charge of the paper. Reporters find out the news stories and write them. The paper is printed so that it is on sale every morning.

The reporter phones the newspaper to tell her story. A typist types it out.

People phone up the editor when something interesting is happening.

Next, the editor decides how much 'space' to give the story. Important stories take up most of a page.

The editor sends a reporter and a photographer to find out more.

The stories are keyed into a computer and made into print.

6

The first copies are called 'proofs'.
A sub-editor corrects mistakes.

7

The stories are all arranged in the
paper. Then the copies are printed.

8

The newspapers are put in vans.
They are taken all over the country.

9

The papers arrive early in the
morning, and people buy them.

10

Not all newspapers come out every
day. Some are Sunday newspapers.
Local newspapers report the news
for different parts of the country.
They are usually printed once a
week. People working on these
papers do not have to work in such
a hurry. Sometimes reporters travel
all over the world to report news.

Working in a hotel

When you go to a hotel, the first person you will see is the receptionist. She will see if there is a room for you, and give you the key. Then a porter will carry your suitcase up to your room. Each room has a different door number.

A chambermaid will clean the room and make the bed. In the restaurant, a waiter will show you a menu. This tells you what food the chef is cooking. When you have chosen your meal, he will write down your order and bring it to you. The wine waiter will bring you wine.

DID YOU KNOW?

Not many buildings have their roofs in the clouds. One building in America is 110 storeys high.

The biggest newspaper in the world is the New York Times. The largest copy published weighed 3 kilos (7½ lbs).

A barber's shop in America employs 60 barbers. This is more than in any other barber's shop.

There's a lady in Britain who knits faster than anyone else. One year she made 885 garments.

Super Book is the name of the world's biggest book. It is 2½ metres (9 ft) high.

Index

190